Returning Cultural Artefacts

Sally Cowan

Contents

Aboriginal and Torres Strait Islander peoples are advised that this text may contain the names and images of people who have died.

Returning Cultural Artefacts

Artefacts and Museums

Museums are interesting places to visit. They have collections of unusual and valuable **artefacts** on display. The artefacts come from different places and cultures around the world. But behind some of the collections is a difficult issue which some museums keep quiet about or **downplay**. It concerns how some of the artefacts came to be in the museums' collections, and whether they should still be held there.

Tourists look at the Rosetta Stone, an ancient Egyptian artefact, in the British Museum.

Many of the artefacts were taken from their homelands during the **colonial era**. This was a period beginning about 500 years ago, when people from Britain and other countries in Europe began to travel more widely. They went on ships to other parts of the world, where they saw ancient artworks and met **First Nations peoples** from many cultures. The Europeans were looking for new items to trade and new lands that Europeans had never visited before. Sometimes, they set up colonies in these lands.

The Europeans saw that life was very different in other parts of the world. They became fascinated with the **cultural** artefacts of these places, such as everyday tools and **ceremonial** items. They also realised that many of the artefacts were valuable works of art. Sometimes, people took artefacts back to Europe for study, or to put them on show to the public there. Other times, they simply wanted them for themselves.

This tiger head is an Indian artefact held in the Clive collection at Powis Castle, Wales.

All sorts of people, including **diplomats**, explorers, traders and soldiers, took artefacts from local people. Sometimes, they traded them for other items or paid small amounts of money for the artefacts. Often, they just stole them.

In the colonial era, European people did not always think about whether it was right or wrong to take artefacts from their original owners. Sometimes, the Europeans believed they were protecting valuable items by removing them. Over time, many of these artefacts were sold to some of the largest, most famous museums in the world. Most of these artefacts have remained in the museums ever since.

Visitors look at First Nations artefacts in the Royal Ontario Museum, Canada.

Many descendants of the original owners of these items have called for the artefacts to be returned to their homelands, often without success. Today, many people have questioned why large foreign museums and private owners still hold the **heritage** of other people in their collections.

The English word **loot** comes from the Hindi word "lut", meaning to steal or plunder. The word became popular in English when Britain controlled India as a colonial power.

Queen Victoria of England wears the Koh-i-Noor diamond, taken from India.

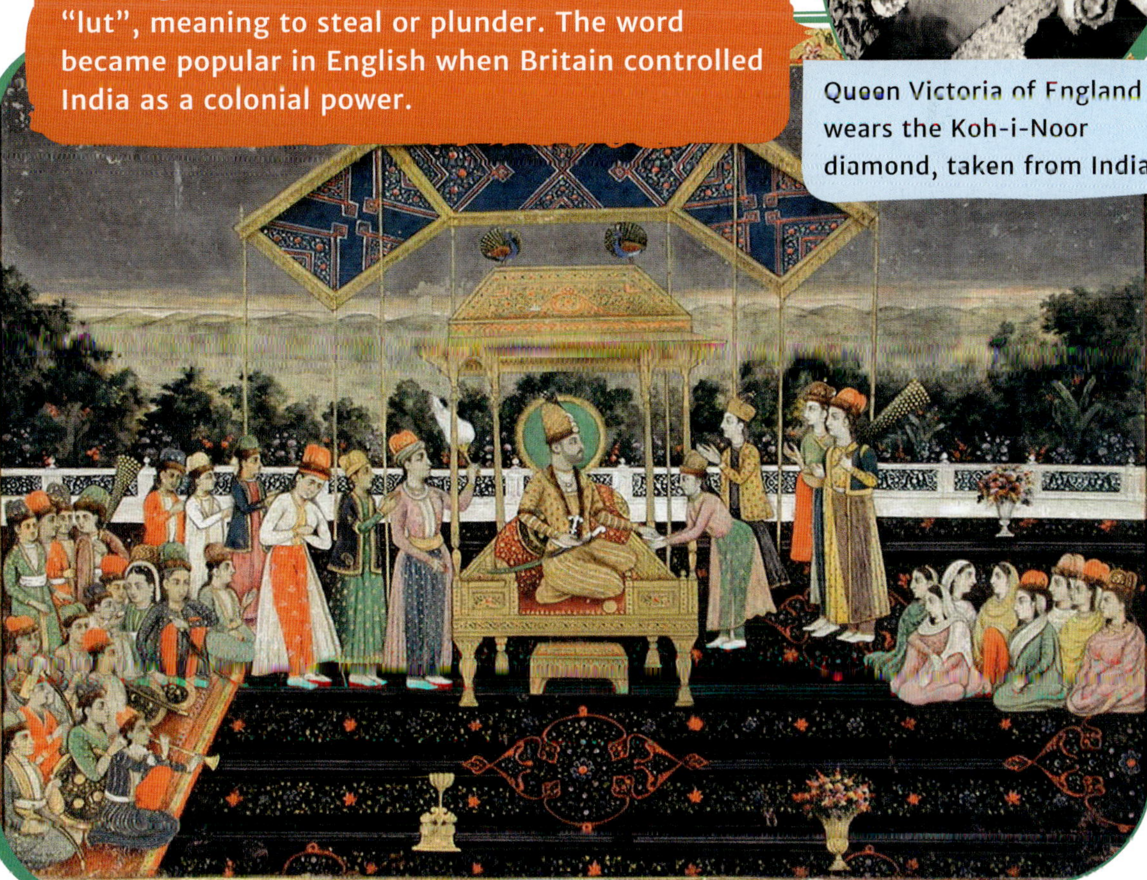

This watercolour artwork from 1850 shows the Peacock Throne, where the Koh-i-Noor diamond once sat as a symbol of Indian rulers.

Returning Artefacts

Returning artefacts to their original owners is not a new idea. More than 2000 years ago, the ancient Greeks wrote about the need for invaders to respect Greek culture. This was after their statues had continually been stolen during wars.

In 1815, one of the first large-scale returns of artefacts occurred. After the French emperor Napoleon was defeated, the leaders of other countries in Europe met to restore order. They forced the French to return thousands of stolen artefacts to their original owners.

The Horses of St Marks in Venice were taken by Napoleon to place on the Arc de Tromphe in Paris.

The French emperor Napoleon was known for taking artefacts from defeated countries.

After World War II, thousands of artworks that had been stolen by German soldiers were found hidden in caves.

Many artefacts were also returned after the two world wars in the twentieth century. But again, this could only happen because the countries that had won the wars could make new rules. They demanded that the governments of the defeated countries return the items they had taken during the war.

By the 1950s, people started to raise the idea that important artefacts taken from First Nations peoples should be returned to them. An organisation called UNESCO encouraged countries to begin a new era of cooperation and fairness in returning artefacts. While many artefacts have been returned since then, there are countless others that haven't been.

UNESCO stands for United Nations Educational, Scientific and Cultural Organization. It continues to encourage the peaceful return of cultural artefacts, and it works to prevent further thefts from occurring.

The Parthenon Sculptures

The British Museum in London, England, is one of the largest museums in the world. In its vast collections are some valuable **marble** sculptures known as the Parthenon Sculptures. They are some of the most famous artefacts to have been taken from their homeland and put on display in another country.

The sculptures were once part of the Parthenon, which is an ancient temple in Athens, Greece. It was built about 2500 years ago. The sculptures come from many parts of the building, but most are from a **frieze** that decorated the top of the temple on all four sides. Since 1983, the Greek government has repeatedly requested that the sculptures be returned to Greece. But the British Museum has refused to return them.

The Parthenon ruins have been carefully preserved and still sit above the city of Athens.

The sculptures were sent to England by Lord Elgin in the early 1800s. Elgin had briefly visited Athens in his role as British **Ambassador** to the Ottoman Empire. At that time, Athens was part of this empire.

The Ottoman Turks had invaded Greece almost 400 years earlier. Many ancient Greek buildings had been damaged during that time. In 1687, a store of **gunpowder** inside the Parthenon was blown up during the fighting, and the Parthenon was left in ruins.

an image of Athena painted on an ancient cup

The Parthenon was built to celebrate the Greek goddess Athena. Its frieze shows a parade of horses, people and other animals that took place every four years to celebrate Athena's birth.

This 1805 painting by Edward Dodwell and Simone Pomardi shows the removal of the Parthenon Sculptures by Lord Elgin in 1801.

By the time Lord Elgin visited Athens, pieces of the marble sculptures were still lying on the ground around the temple. Elgin knew how rare and valuable the ancient sculptures were. In 1801, he asked the Ottoman **sultan** for permission to take some of them to England. Elgin said that he wanted to protect them from further damage. The sultan gave permission for pieces of stone to be removed. For several years afterwards, Elgin organised the shipping of the sculptures to London, where he put them on display. Crowds of people came to marvel at the ancient artworks.

In this 1819 painting by Archibald Archer, the Parthenon Sculptures are displayed to a wealthy crowd in a temporary room at the British Museum.

In 1816, Elgin sold the Parthenon Sculptures to the British Museum. Even at the time, there was discussion about whether these Greek artefacts should be returned to the Parthenon in Athens. By then, Athens was back under Greek rule. But the museum officials chose to buy the sculptures. They then put them on display to the public in 1832. They have been in the British Museum ever since.

The sculptures have also been called the Parthenon Marbles, because the sculptures are made of marble.

People can see the Parthenon Sculptures that were taken by Lord Elgin in the British Museum today.

For many years, the British Museum and the Greek government have disagreed about who owns the sculptures. British Museum officials have said that the sculptures belong in the museum because Elgin acquired them honestly to preserve them. But the Greek government says that the sculptures belong to Greece. They point out that the Ottoman sultan was an invader, who had no right to give away Greek heritage. Also, the sultan only gave Elgin permission to take pieces of stone that were lying on the ground, but Elgin's workers sawed large chunks of marble off the temple, including the frieze. The Greeks say that he was dishonest and caused even more damage to the ancient temple.

Greek protesters call for the return of the Parthenon Sculptures, also called the Marbles, in 2018.

In the Acropolis Museum, missing parts of the frieze have been filled with white plaster replicas.

In 2009, the Greek government opened a **state-of-the-art** museum near the Parthenon to display some of its remaining sculptures. They were moved from the Parthenon to protect them from damage caused by pollution and **weathering**. A special gallery in the museum displays the remains of the frieze. It clearly shows that more than half of the frieze is missing because it is in the British Museum. The display was designed to send a powerful message to museum-goers. And after seeing it, many of them think that the whole frieze should be displayed in the ancient city where it was built.

There may finally be a change coming. The British Museum and the Greek government began talks in 2021. It is possible that they will agree to share these, and other, sculptures.

The Acropolis Museum in Athens displays the remaining Parthenon Sculptures that were not taken by Lord Elgin.

The Benin Bronzes

A Benin bronze wall plaque shows a bird.

In 2022, the German government announced that German museums would return valuable artefacts that were stolen from Nigeria. The artefacts are part of a collection known as the Benin Bronzes. They include sculptures and wall **plaques** made from **bronze**, brass and wood that tell the history of an African kingdom. These artworks were crafted over 600 years ago in the Kingdom of Benin, which was located in present-day Nigeria.

In 1897, British soldiers attacked Benin City after a disagreement with the oba, or king, of Benin. He had wanted to restrict British trade in the area. In the attack, the British soldiers looted thousands of artefacts from the Benin Royal Palace. The palace was destroyed, and the oba was forced to leave his country.

British troops pose with large piles of stolen artefacts in Benin City, 1897.

In the early 1900s, many of the British soldiers sold the stolen artefacts in art auctions. The artefacts were bought by several large museums in European countries. Soon after, people from Benin City unsuccessfully called for the return of their artefacts. Then, in the 1970s, some Nigerians tried to reclaim them, but again without success.

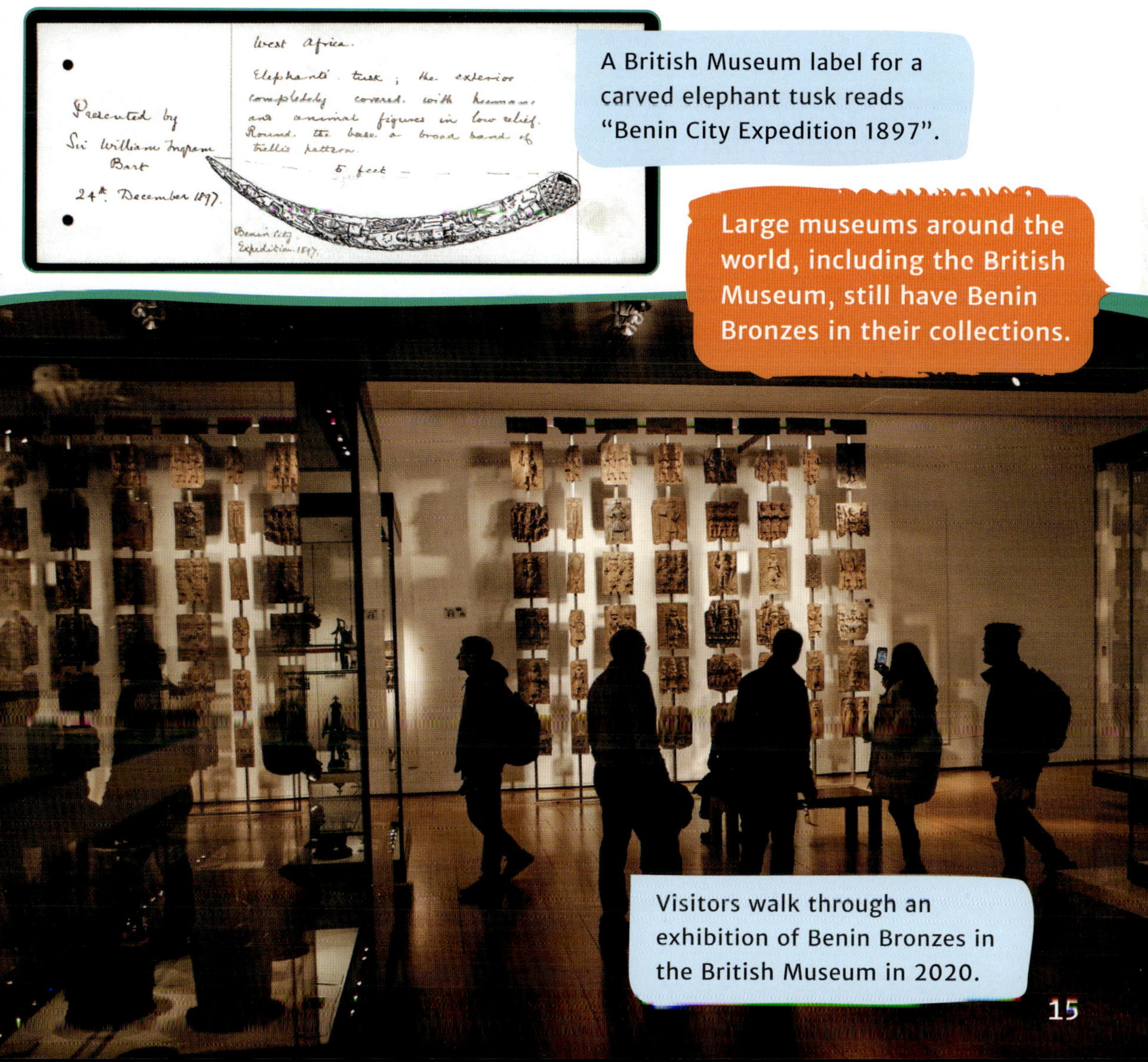

A British Museum label for a carved elephant tusk reads "Benin City Expedition 1897".

Large museums around the world, including the British Museum, still have Benin Bronzes in their collections.

Visitors walk through an exhibition of Benin Bronzes in the British Museum in 2020.

In 2018, the **attitudes** of some politicians and museum officials in Europe began to change. The president of France announced that France would return artworks stolen from its former colonies in Africa. The German government also began talks with the Nigerians about returning the Benin Bronzes held in German museums.

In total, five German museums had over 1000 artefacts to return to Nigeria. It is the biggest number of artefacts ever to be returned. The museum officials from both countries worked together. As a result, the Nigerians agreed to leave some items on loan to German museums.

Germany's Foreign Minister and the Nigerian Minister of Culture stand with some Benin Bronzes after the agreement to return them in 2022.

In Nigeria, many people were excited about the return of these Benin Bronzes. They saw it as a way to learn more about their culture and history. Others wanted **compensation** for the hurt and wrongs of the past. As a supportive gesture, the German government agreed to partly pay for a museum in Nigeria to display the returned Benin Bronzes.

A bronze plaque shows the oba of Benin with two helpers.

The wall plaques of the Benin Bronzes show scenes of life in the palace of the Kingdom of Benin. They are an important source of historical and cultural information for the people of Nigeria.

Returning First Nations Artefacts

Like the Nigerians, other First Nations peoples have called for the return of their ancestors' cultural items. There are special groups set up in countries such as Australia and Aotearoa New Zealand to help Australian First Nations and Māori peoples find cultural artefacts held in museums around the world. The following two examples show what can be achieved with cooperation.

Students learn about Canadian First Nations artefacts in an exhibition created with help from First Nations groups at the Museum of Anthropology, Canada.

The Australian Institute of Aboriginal and Torres Strait Islander Studies (AIATSIS) holds discussions with museums on behalf of First Nations peoples. In 2021, the organisation managed the return of over 1800 ancient First Nations tools from the Israel Museum. The stone tools belonged to a Jewish man, who had been fascinated by First Nations culture. He had collected the tools in the mid-twentieth century. Then, he donated his collection to the Israel Museum in the 1970s.

The members of AIATSIS helped the Israel Museum staff to identify and study the tools. The museum's director wanted to be respectful to First Nations culture and heritage. So, he agreed to return the collection to Australia.

These Wurundjeri Woi-Wurrung stone tools held by the Israel Museum were returned to traditional owners in Australia in 2022.

In New Zealand in 2017, there was an exhibition of Māori artefacts which included items from several museums around the world. The exhibition was created by the local Māori **iwi**, which provided funding for a researcher to locate the artefacts.

One unexpected find was a carved ceremonial club, known as the wahaika. Its location had been unknown to Māori people for 100 years until the researcher discovered it in the Fowler Museum at the University of California, Los Angeles.

The rare wahaika had belonged to a Māori leader. After his death, his wife gave it to the governor of New Zealand as a gift before the governor's return to England. The wahaika was later sold in an auction and was lost to history. While it was not returned to New Zealand permanently, it was loaned to the exhibition by the university. The wahaika was welcomed back to New Zealand with a traditional Māori greeting and cultural ceremonies.

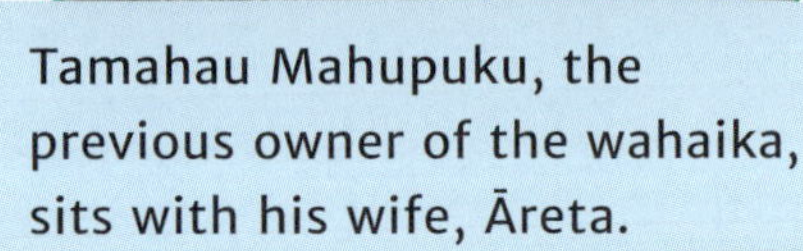

Tamahau Mahupuku, the previous owner of the wahaika, sits with his wife, Āreta.

The wahaika was created by Jacob Heberley, a skilled carver of Te Atiawa descent.

University researcher Kevin Tibbett (right) returns a collection of artefacts to Kalkadoon elder Richard Percy in 2002.

After difficult times in the past, many museums are finding ways to cooperate with people from different cultures. The return of cultural artefacts to their homelands seems to be entering a more respectful phase. It is exciting to think about what other artefacts might be returned in the future.

Should Cultural Artefacts Be Returned?

In the past, cultural artefacts were taken from First Nations peoples around the world. Many of these artefacts are now in large museums in Europe and the USA. Today, a growing number of people think that the artefacts should be returned to the descendants of their original owners. I agree that this should happen. But some people, including my uncle, think that the artefacts should stay in museums.

Noura

This bust of the ancient Egyptian queen Nefertiti, held by the Neues Museum in Berlin, Germany, was illegally taken out of Egypt in 1913.

Many people believe that returning the artefacts could help to fix mistakes made in the past. Today, people know that some cruel and unfair events happened to First Nations people in the colonial era. Many artefacts were taken from them without their permission.

For example, on Captain James Cook's first voyage exploring the east coast of Australia, his crew stole about forty spears. They belonged to the Gweagal people of the Eora Nation in New South Wales. The spears were taken back to England to be studied as **curiosities** of an ancient culture. However, the theft of so many spears must have caused serious problems for the Gweagal people. They needed the spears to catch fish and other foods.

These spears were taken from the Gweagal people by Captain James Cook in 1770.

My uncle argues that returning artefacts can't make up for harms done to people in the past, because these events happened so long ago and the people are no longer alive. He believes it would be hard to find the descendants of the original owners. Often, not much is known about where artefacts came from. Furthermore, he says that the museums usually paid for the artefacts at the time they acquired them, so the museums own the artefacts and there is no need to return them.

Millions of tourists visit the Louvre museum in France every year.

However, there are special organisations that help people to find their ancestors' artefacts. So, I believe many items could be returned. People should be able to display their heritage in their own country. Not everyone can afford to travel to distant museums to see and learn about their own culture. What makes this issue even worse is that a huge number of artefacts are locked away in storage in the large museums, where no one at all can see them. Instead of locking them away, First Nations peoples could reconnect with their ancestors' treasured items.

This Rapa Nui (Easter Island) moai is kept in the British Museum, thousands of kilometres away from its traditional owners.

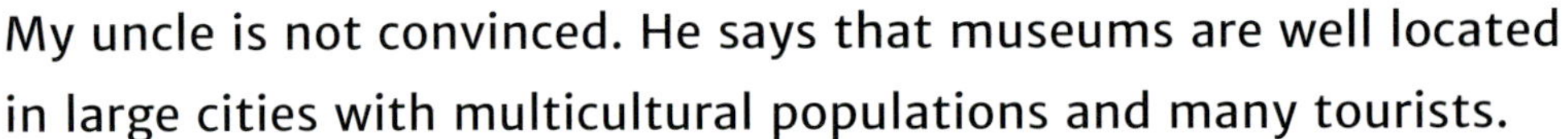

My uncle is not convinced. He says that museums are well located in large cities with multicultural populations and many tourists. This gives large numbers of people the chance to see artefacts from a range of cultures all brought together in one place. He says that visiting museums helps people learn about other cultures and respect them. While he agrees it is unfortunate that many artefacts are in storage, he believes that large museums have the best facilities for preserving artefacts.

This game board from the city of Ur is kept in the British Museum.

The ancient Sumerian city of Ur is located in modern-day Iraq and is not safe for tourists to visit.

Finally, I think there could be benefits for museums that work with the descendants of original owners. The descendants might not want to have all of their ancestors' artefacts returned, but they appreciate being asked. When items do get returned to their homelands, the museum officials can build good relationships with the local people. This might mean that the museums are able to borrow other cultural items for displaying in special exhibitions.

The Temple of Dendur (now in the Metropolitan Museum of Art in New York City) was given to the USA by Egypt after the USA helped to save the ancient structure from destruction.

But my uncle is concerned that museums could lose a lot of their exhibitions. He enjoys visiting museums and believes that if some had to close down, it would take away an interesting pastime. In addition, he says that museum **curators** have saved artefacts that would probably have been thrown away, lost or broken. So, museums can be important protectors of different cultures.

A museum technician works to carefully restore an Indigenous Central American artefact.

While museums may have helped to preserve artefacts, this doesn't mean that they should keep them in the future. If nothing is done to try to fix the harms that happened in the past, they will continue to upset many First Nations peoples. That is why more and more people think, like I do, that returning artefacts is the best way to show respect for other peoples' cultures.

Bermagui man Rodney Kelly argues for the return of his ancestor's Gweagal shield in the British Museum in 2018.

Glossary

ambassador (*noun*)	someone sent by a government to represent their country in another place
artefacts (*noun*)	objects made by people, usually connected with their culture
attitudes (*noun*)	ways people think and feel about things
bronze (*noun*)	a brownish metal that is a mixture of copper and tin
ceremonial (*adjective*)	used for special events
colonial era (*noun*)	a time when many powerful European countries controlled other countries outside Europe
compensation (*noun*)	payment in return for damage that has occurred
cooperation (*noun*)	working together towards a shared goal
cultural (*adjective*)	to do with the customs and traditions of a group of people
curators (*noun*)	people who are in charge of the objects in a museum or gallery
curiosities (*noun*)	strange, interesting and unusual objects
diplomats (*noun*)	people who work for their governments in another country
downplay (*verb*)	to make something seem less important

First Nations peoples (*noun*)
the first peoples living in an area

frieze (*noun*) a sculpted decoration along the top border of a building or room

gunpowder (*noun*) explosive powder used in bombs

heritage (*noun*) the history, items, traditions and customs important to a country or society

iwi (*noun*) a Māori nation or large related group of people

loot (*verb*) to steal in times of war or disaster

marble (*noun*) a hard, usually white stone that can be sculpted

plaques (*noun*) flat pieces of metal or stone recording a piece of history

state-of-the-art (*adjective*)
modern, using the latest technology

sultan (*noun*) a king or ruler

weathering (*noun*) damage caused by wind, rain and sun over time

Index